# THE IDIAT AND THE ODD-YSSEY

## THE ADVENTURES OF ODYFFERUS
## THROUGH INTERNATIONAL GEORGIA

### HARLAN HAMBRIGHT

# THE IDIAT AND THE ODD-YSSEY
## THE ADVENTURES OF ODYFFERUS THROUGH INTERNATIONAL GEORGIA

COPYRIGHT © 2010 BY HARLAN HAMBRIGHT

MARY BRAY WHEELER, EDITOR

PUBLISHED BY CRAWDAD STUDIO & GALLERY
ST. SIMONS ISLAND, GEORGIA

PRINTED BY THE HARTLEY PRESS
JACKSONVILLE, FLORIDA

## WWW.THEIDIAT.COM

### ABOUT THE AUTHOR

Harlan Hambright is an architectural photographer and graphic designer based on St. Simons Island off the coast of Georgia. He is also a partner in H$_2$O Creative Group, an ad agency and design shop similarly located. He received a Bachelor of Architecture degree from the University of Tennessee in 1976, lived in Washington, D.C. from 1980-1990 before relocating to the Georgia coast. Previous books include *Coast Cottages*, a 2003 book about the Coastal Living Idea House, *The Cloister*, a pictorial tour of Sea Island's new upscale hotel, and *The Art of the Cloister*, a descriptive catalogue of the Cloister's extensive collection. He has been widely published in various trade magazines and books over the years and resides with his wife, Rhonda, one of the finest sopranos east of the Mississippi River.

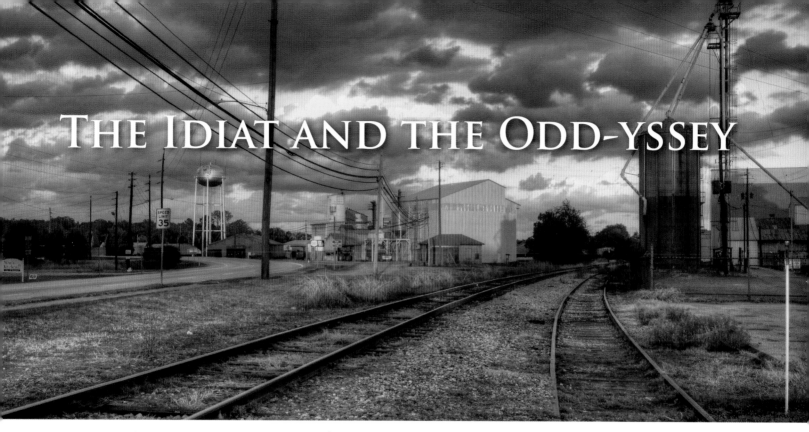

# THE IDIAT AND THE ODD-YSSEY

## ACKNOWLEDGMENTS

Thanks to all my state-wide clients whose assignments allowed me to travel all around Georgia pursuing this project, several members of St. Simons Presbyterian Church who called my attention to places I had missed, all the cooperative folks I encountered along the way, my H$_2$O family, Rhonda, my friend and conceptual artist Irwin Berman, and Mary Bray Wheeler, a very thorough editor.

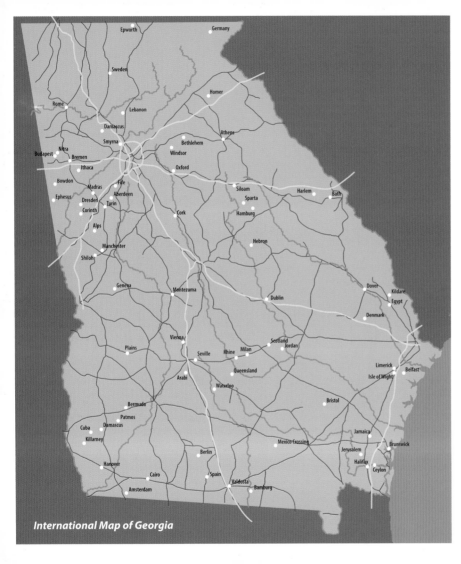

**International Map of Georgia**

# INTERNATIONAL GEORGIA

A map, left, of the 70 international locations Odyfferus was able to locate and visit. There are approximately seven hundred cities, towns and villages in the state, so this represents ten percent of them, roughly.

The red lines indicate railroads and reveal how important rail was to the development of many, if not most of the communities contained herein (if not the entire state itself). Yellow lines represent interstate highways which, as you can see, are not very useful in touring the world in Georgia. If you do make this journey, you will see many miles of two lane roads and not a few dirt roads.

Making a similar journey using the map to the right would be fairly costly, though much more interesting.

Other identified locations (mostly former locations), not included herein for one reason or another include:

| | | |
|---|---|---|
| Aberdeen | Dartmouth | Montevideo |
| Acton | Fife | New Holland |
| Antioch | Hebron | New Switzerland |
| Bamberg | Lisbon | Paris |
| Birmingham | Lodi | Quebec |
| Buena Vista | Macedonia | Tyre |
| Cyrene | Mexico Crossing | Winchester |

# Introduction and Apologies

*The generation of men is like that of leaves. The wind scatters one year's leaves on the ground, but the forest burgeons and puts out others, as the season of spring comes round. So it is with men: one generation grows on, and another is passing away.*

—Homer, *The Iliad*

Whatever else the present work may be, it is a sometimes melancholy documentary of Homer's observation at work here in Georgia. As we proceed headlong into the twenty-first century and as a new generation "grows on," evidence of previous generations—primarily railroad- and agriculture-oriented communities—are being treated as so many leaves lying on the ground. Bypassed and ignored, once-thriving towns are literally crumbling apart. This project is not a criticism of that process, just an acknowledgment and record of it. On the other hand, a few communities continue to prosper culturally and renovate their building stock in spite of economic circumstances and one must wonder what the differences are: community pride? visionary leadership? something in the water? or are there other economic forces at work?

I first got the idea for this project a couple of years before the 1996 Olympics held in Atlanta. "Wouldn't it be clever to present Georgia as an international melting pot and photograph little towns in the same heroic manner one would document, say, St. Peter's Basilica?" I thought. Owing to many factors, the idea unfortunately lost steam and lay dormant until now. The twenty-first century world is now ready. I combed the index of my Georgia Gazetteer and identified over sixty locations which seemed to be named after international sites. I missed a few, partly owing to eyesight, and partly owing to ignorance—how was I supposed to know that Valdosta was named after the Italian *Valle d'Aosta* for example. Diligent searching revealed a few more and all of them should be here. If I missed your community, I either apologize or you should consider yourself lucky.

*It is tedious to tell again tales already plainly told.*

—Homer, *The Odyssey*

Once again, my mentor, Dr. Homer, is right. Therefore, I endeavor to tell a new tale, poorly disguised as an old one. I am combining my nearly forty years of experience as a photographer, my appreciation of architecture and history, and an inherited sense of humor to create what I desperately hope you will find to be an informative, interesting, and entertaining artifact. I am aware of the difficulty in categorizing the work. A small portion has appeared serially in *Golden Isles Magazine* published in Brunswick, Georgia, and has been found offensive by a few. I am not making fun of anyone: if I say there's nothing to do in Amsterdam, it's because, well, there's nothing to do in Amsterdam, and give me a break—I do present the actual history of its founding.

As an architectural photographer, I have found it quite interesting to compare present day design philosophies and construction techniques with those of a century or more ago. In general, the legacy we are currently leaving will not speak too highly of us in a few decades. But then you come across a project like the brand new library in Ephesus and realize that maybe there's hope after all.

Forgive me, dear reader, for not reporting this account in dactylic hexameter—I have a hard enough time getting a cogent sentence cobbled together. And I rather doubt that this little project will rise to the level nor achieve the status of Odysseus's adventures. I frankly hope not to encounter a Cyclops, nor be shipwrecked repeatedly. I don't leave a dog behind, and the only siren song I anticipate hearing would be the occasional fire truck or ambulance as I drive from town to town.

This particular *Odd-yssey* is organized by time period first, then global geographical region. We will explore the ironic connections that link us together with other people across vast expanses of time and space, as well as the actual histories of the naming of Georgia's "International" communities. Much of the information regarding the origins of the naming of these communities came from *Georgia Place-Names* by Kenneth K. Krakow, first published in 1975. Additional contemporary information was found in the *Cyclopedia of Georgia* published in 1906 by the State Historical Association and accessed online through Google Books.

We will appropriately begin the adventure in the Classic Period. Before we embark, however, it would be appropriate to turn our attention to Ithaca, the birthplace of Odysseus.

# THE CLASSIC PERIOD

There is some dispute among scholars, interpreting Homer's description of the island of Ithaca, over the true identity of Odysseus's home. Today's Ithaca is a forty-five-square-mile island in the Ionian Sea in Greece. The nearby islands of Echinades, Leukas and the western peninsula of Kefalonia, believed to once have been an island, now known as Paliki, are all claimed by various authorities to be the true location of Homer's Ithaca. Regardless, it is safe to say that Georgia's Ithaca does not have a dog in the hunt. If Odysseus were from Ithaca, Georgia, he would certainly have left, as he did, but probably would not have bothered to return.

Information regarding the history and naming of Ithaca, Georgia (the home of Odyfferus), is difficult to come by. It does figure heavily, however, as a primary location in the 2006 novel *Revenge of the Kudzu Debutantes* by Cathy Holton.

The possibilities of the unknown beckon, so with an unbridled spirit of adventure, Odyfferus casts off (at speeds sometimes exceeding sixty mph!). Since much has been borrowed in the creation of this project from a well-known early author, it is only fitting that we continue our journey in . . .

*The above photograph shows Ithaca's efficient way-finding graphic system.*

*A unique combination of architectural elements greets the sunrise in Ithaca, opposite.*

ITHACA

# HOMER

To pay respects, I was on hand for the fiftieth consecutive running of what was once billed as "The World's Largest Easter Egg Hunt" in Homer, a bit north of Athens, Georgia.

The anticipation of the 2:00 p.m. start of the event, held on Easter Sunday, rivaled that of any major sporting event, the Kentucky Derby, say, or perhaps the Georgia-Florida football game. The crowd grew and grew, surrounding the fence around the several acre pasture on the Garrison farm, and by 1:45 was sizeable and growing restless. As the announcer made the introductions, some impatient treasure

seekers stormed through the gates before the official go-ahead. Anarchy! Thousands of people of all ages wandered through the grass looking for their share of the alleged $10,000 worth of cellophane-wrapped candy eggs scattered amongst the ant hills and cow patties as well as the 100 special eggs designating a special treat, a live bunny for example. Everyone seemed to be having a good time.

To be perfectly honest, from a historical perspective however, the town of Homer, incorporated in 1859, was actually named after one Homer Jackson, an early settler.

*Right:* a young egg hunter endears himself to strangers.

*Far right and opposite page:* various scenes of Homer including the new Banks County Courthouse which contrasts dramatically with the pre-existing architecture stock.

# Smyrna

We continue our homage to Homer by paying a call to Smyrna, his birthplace and port on the Aegean. It got its start in the eleventh century BC and was the second city of the seven churches of the Revelation to receive a message from the apostle John.

Smyrna, Georgia, was originally named for a friend of a railroad engineer, Neal Dow, and has been known also as Varner's Station. Its current name was derived from a nearby campground which took its name from, of course, Homer's hometown.

Part of the seemingly never-ending megalopolis of Atlanta, Smyrna has become a desirable community in which to live and has made inroads in new urban planning concepts of mixed-use development based on traditional city models, but with actual parking in the back. The only obvious visual reference of note to its Greek architectural heritage is the arc column contraption pictured on the opposite page.

Also pictured is a typical Smyrnian single family dwelling. Note the Doric column which takes its reference from classical Greek architecture and the city symbol referenced above. Please disregard the human in the chair. That is Blake. He is a nice guy, but in this context, a distracting foreground element.

# ATHENS

Our travel through the Classic period brings us now to Athens. Georgia's Athens, "The Classic City," recently celebrated its 200th anniversary. Athens, in Greece, has been continuously inhabited for over 4500 years—a little perspective for you. Its name was selected by either the trustees of the University of Georgia or the postmaster, whichever you choose to believe. Georgia's Athens has gone a little overboard, architecturally speaking, if you ask me, on the theme of classic Greek design. There must be a covenant that requires any new building to resemble a Greek temple. There are more columns in Athens than in the Sunday *New York Times* for Zeus's sake. Athena, the Greek goddess and protector of our hero, Odysseus, is the namesake of Athens.

The English poet John Milton declared Athens to be the mother of arts and eloquence. A case could be made for Georgia's being, if not the actual mother, at least an aunt of arts and eloquence, though not on a Saturday during football season.

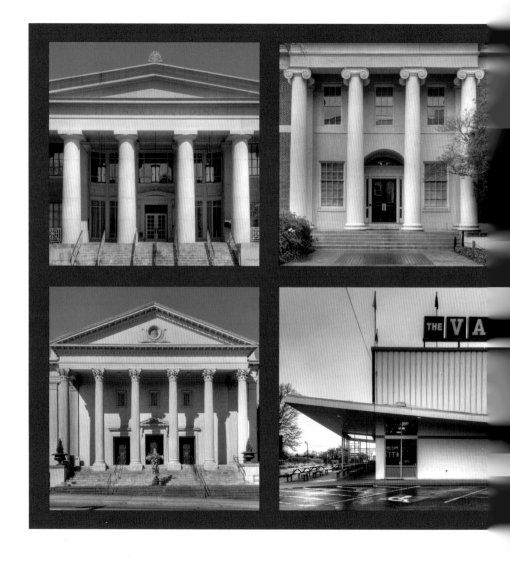

# THE ORDERS

*Athens, Georgia, is a living museum for studying the history of Greek architecture. Shown opposite are excellent examples of the four classical orders: Doric, Ionic, Corinthian, and Cheeseburger with Fries.*

# ROME

In spite of UGA alumni's affinity for Athens, Rome, Georgia, deserves the most attention as a Classic city from a historical perspective. Rome was founded by Romulus and Remus, twin brothers begot by Rhea Silvia, a Vestal Virgin, and Mars, the god of war. Legend has it that Romulus slew his brother so he could become the first King of Rome. Legend is incorrect in this instance, and the record is set straight herewith. In truth, Remus, as is clearly depicted in the photograph of the famous statue (opposite page) was sucking hind teat. (He's the one on the right.) Sucking hind teat don't get you king, so Remus acquiesced and moved eastward, eventually finding himself in the hamlet of Eatonton. When Romulus had a child, Remus became the uncle for which he is famed. This fact is clearly indicated in the accompanying photograph. Remus had obviously gravitated from lupine to lapine as his species of choice, perhaps as a result of geography, if not good taste.

Georgia's Rome was first incorporated in 1834, achieved the status of city in 1847, and was captured by that William Tecumseh Sherman ~~bas~~ fellow just prior to his Atlanta campaign. Like its Italian counterpart, it was built on seven hills and even has a river running through it and those characteristics pretty much describe why Rome is called Rome.

When in Rome . . . Actual Romans partake in their custom of enjoying a family meal in an actual Italian restaurant on a Sunday afternoon. Right: the Coliseum.

# EPHESUS

Our journey brings us next to Ephesus, named after the famed Ionian city mentioned in the Book of Revelation and recipient of the epistle, traditionally credited to Paul, which, greatly simplified, encourages Christians to get along with each other. Now located in Turkey, just thirty-five miles from Smyrna, the original Ephesus was the site of the Celsus Library, completed in 117 AD, which housed some 12,000 scrolls. A casual drive through our Ephesus offers no reason to linger. Get off the beaten track however and the erudite traveler will be utterly flabbergasted by the fact that the Ephesians recently held the grand opening of—are you sitting down?—their new library! A volunteer stocking the shelves told me they had been fund-raising and planning this for over ten years and that before they had to travel fifteen miles to the nearest library which is odd as it's fifteen miles to *anything*. This just demonstrates what a community can accomplish with dedication and determination, if not a little help from the General Assembly.

Just three or four miles away from Veal, Roosterville, and neighboring Alabama, the present Ephesus was not incorporated until 1964 AD.

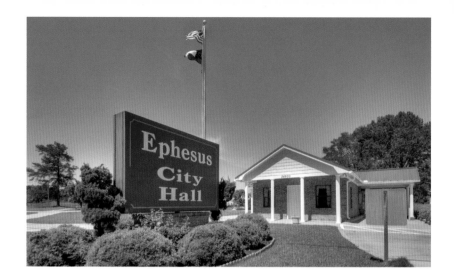

# Sparta

In 478 BC, Ephesus joined with Athens and Sparta and formed the Delian League, so let's turn our attention to Sparta.

Sparta emerged as a political entity around the tenth century BC. It was the dominant military power in ancient Greece from c. 650 BC until its defeat by Thebes in 371 BC.

Our Sparta, seat of Hancock County, was incorporated in 1805. It was named by a Revolutionary War Major to reflect the bravery of its citizens. Once, quite the thriving town, it, along with Athens, helped to inspire the Greek Revival in Georgia. Today, however, it is rather, well, spartan.

Ancient Sparta was very much a militaristic state. Mothers of newborns would bathe their babies in wine to see if they were strong. If the infant survived, the father would bring it before the Gerousia (a Spartan council of elders) who decided if it would be reared or not. If it was considered "puny and deformed," it was thrown into a chasm on Mount Taygetos. There is absolutely no evidence to suggest that this sort of practice has ever been considered in Sparta, Georgia.

# CORINTH

Sparta faced a conflict with Corinth beginning in 395 BC. Georgia's Corinth, not that far from Ephesus, was named for the Greek one for no other reason than they both are at a crossroads. Corinth enjoyed a very high standard of living for its day—think of Beverly Hills or, more locally, Sea Island or Buckhead. Horace, Rome's leading lyric poet at the end of BC, once said, in Latin presumably, "Not everyone is able to go to Corinth." The same could be said of today's Corinth, but for different reasons altogether.

In Paul's first Epistle to the Corinthians, he reflects on the difficulty of maintaining a Christian community in a cosmopolitan environment. A similar sentiment would be wasted on today's Corinth. It is loaded with churches and an urban, indulgent culture is not present to distract the faithful.

The opposite page depicts a Corinthian outdoor market. (Actually, Corinth's only market.)

HOT
BOILED P-NUT

nts & Garden Center

# Damascus

Damascus, Syria, is one of the oldest continually populated places on Earth and was the terminus for three caravan routes. It is difficult to write about Damascus, Georgia, because I do not know what the plural of Damascus is. Suffice it to say that for whatever reason, there are two of them. That they are named after the Syrian capital is well documented. Why is another matter altogether.

The southernmost one, in Early County, relies on peanut processing while the more northern one, in Gordon County, doesn't really seem to have that much going for it except for a small company that sells old mail and ice cream trucks.

The Early County one was previously someplace else but they moved it to its present location when the railroad station was built and the post office opened there. It may not be here much longer if someone doesn't move in and prop up some of its buildings.

*Above:* North Damascus yard art.

*Left:* East across the Arabian desert from Damascus is Babylon, home of the Hanging Gardens. Could this be Georgia's historical nod to a Seven Wonder (rendered in kudzu)?

*Opposite:* Wash day in Damascus.

# PLAINS

"Nebuchadnezzar the king made an image of gold, whose height was threescore cubits, and the breadth thereof six cubits: he set it up in the plain of Dura, in the province of Babylon," begins the third chapter of the Book of Daniel. A few verses later Nebuchadnezzar commands everyone to bow down to this image. This is where Shadrach, Meshach, and Abednego refuse and are thrown into a very hot furnace but are not consumed. This impresses Nebuchadnezzar no end causing him to change his mind about matters regarding the nature of gods, theirs especially, and to give Shadrach, Meshach, and Abednego promotions.

Plains, Georgia, was named for Plains of Dura, a nearby spot with a post office which, like many other early Georgia communities, picked up and moved when the railroad was built. Plains of Dura (Georgia) had been named for Plain of Dura (Bible) and the plural designation is but a matter of conjecture. This particular area of southeast Georgia is quite level which could suggest a plain to some, and the Plain of Dura specifically to others.

In Plains there is an image of peanut whose height is some eight and a half cubits, and the breadth thereof three cubits. There is no evidence suggesting that anything as noteworthy as people surviving cremation in a furnace has occurred near this icon. It is a caricature of a nearby resident, the thirty-ninth president of the United States no less which, upon reflection, *is* rather noteworthy.

# Patmos

I went to Patmos seeking a revelation. In this regard I was disappointed. Why would people creating a new community, in 1839, many miles away from any significant body of water, decide to name it after the Greek island where John supposedly received the vision from Christ which ultimately resulted in the last book of the New Testament? (There are many arguments regarding the true identity of this John and interpretations of this particular Bible book, but all that is outside the scope of the present work.) What is not controversial is that the "former hamlet," Patmos, will no time soon become a major tourist destination. Kenneth Krakow even cites the desolation of the area as the genesis of the name Patmos.

The Bible, however, does make a cameo appearance here. A sign, at the intersection of Julia Jones Road and Route 216, points the way and announces, "Burning Bush, 5 miles." The location of the writing of the last book of the Bible makes a direct connection to a major occurrence in the second book of the Bible. Therefore, one could extrapolate, based on empirical evidence in southwest Georgia, that the Bible is just over five miles long which just further adds to the enigma of the Book of Revelation. I leave it to others to further speculation about and confirmation of this wobbly supposition.

# JORDAN

Jordan is a country in the Middle East which, along with Israel and the Palestinian Authority, shares control of the Dead Sea, the lowest dry land point on the planet. It contains within its borders several UNESCO World Heritage sites including the city of Petra, established sometime in the sixth century BC and literally carved from the rocks in a basin on the slope of Mount Hor. The BBC lists it in "the 40 places you have to see before you die."

In contrast, Jordan, Georgia, lies 236 feet above sea level and is the site of a small, now-closed gas station dating from the early- to mid-twentieth century AD and an all-but-abandoned school campus from around the same period. It is one of the rare Georgia communities for which little-to-no historical information seems to exist.

# BETHLEHEM

Oh, how we can see the little town of Bethlehem lying still near Loganville, just northeast of Atlanta. It was incorporated in 1902 and was built on the Gainesville, Jefferson & Southern railway. It is now billed as "The Christmas Town of Georgia." You enter the town from the north on Christmas Avenue and can turn onto Wise Men Lane, Angel or Manger Avenues, or Mary, Joseph, or Star Streets. There is a Post Office here which does a brisk business in December canceling stamps.

The town was named after the Methodist church and camp of the same name which just predate the Civil War. The predominant architectural style of the town does not make any reference whatsoever to its biblical heritage—it is mildly Victorian, a period not generally associated with the original Nativity.

Georgia enjoys other hamlets associated with the New Testament. One, Jerusalem, is located in Camden County near Woodbine, so let's continue our journey there.

*Dante's Inferno is not generally associated with the little town of Bethlehem, but that's what comes to mind by autumn lawn maintenance, right.*

*Though it has not been confirmed by biblical scholars nor archaeologists, this modest structure found in the middle of Bethlehem could well be the manger or, at worst, a well executed counterfeit.*

# Jerusalem

Jerusalem, the controversial capital of present-day Israel, enjoys a history spanning nearly six thousand years, making it one of the oldest cities in the world. It is Judaism's spiritual center, is quite significant in Christianity, and is the third holiest city in Islam. Jerusalem, Georgia's, religious significance would appear to be limited to the presence of a modestly attended Baptist Church. A suburb, if you will, of Woodbine in nearby Camden County, its historical information is hard to come by. Bailey's Mill, an early settlement, was located here and the Bartram Trail, named for eighteenth-century naturalist William Bartram's southern journey from March, 1773, to January, 1777, passes close by.

# SHILOH

Shiloh, Georgia, seems to have gotten its start as a train stop just before 1900. It was not incorporated until 1961 and was named for the local Baptist church which took its name from the biblical city of Shiloh in Ephraim, a very popular location in the Old Testamant. It was the religious capital of Israel during the Book of Judges era. It is where Moses directed a tent to be made to house the Ark of the Covenant. Shiloh makes cameo appearances in Joshua, Samuel, Psalms, and Jeremiah. Shiloh, Georgia, is not mentioned in the Bible, nor any other major publications known to this writer.

# SILOAM

Siloam got its start in the early 1840s as Smyrna. The post office department requested a new name since there was already a Smyrna and the residents elected to use the biblical name from the Tunnel of Siloam, used by Hezekiah in the defense of Jerusalem. The 533 meter-long tunnel, built before 701 BC, served as an aquaduct to supply water to the ancient city of Jerusalem during the anticipated seige by the Assyrians.

One may walk the tunnel today from end to end. One may more easily walk Siloam, Georgia, from end to end, but to be brutally frank, there is not much to see, unless you count the multiple *water towers* which ironically supply water to the town, though there are hopefully no seiges planned for the near future.

# THE EAST

## EGYPT

Egypt, Georgia, began as a 1572-acre plantation purchased in 1870 by Confederate General Lafayette McLaws. His daughter Virginia wrote that it was so-named because of the fine corn that was grown there. It was later on the main line of the Central of Georgia railroad and was apparently an important shipping point two turns of the century ago, at which time it boasted a population of 250.

It is situated between Statesboro and Ebenezer, the historic spot (and second English settlement in Georgia) where the Salzburgers took up residence back in 1734.

It currently offers little to beckon the weary traveler to linger.

# CAIRO

The obvious connection of Cairos would be the pyramid and there are no shortages of these in Cairo, Georgia, though one must use one's imagination.

Cairo, named for either its counterpart in Egypt or Illinois (probably the former), was a railroad shipping center and, at the beginning of the twentieth century, had become the center for the syrup trade in the state, which leads to another one of those strange quirks of history: Cairo, nicknamed the syrup city, is mispronounced *Karo* (the trade name of a syrup made from corn starch invented by the Corn Products Refining Company of New York and Chicago), and those two things have absolutely nothing to do with one another. How is that possible?

It must have been quite the bustling place in 1900 with a population of 4400. The famous sports persons, Jackie Robinson and Teresa Edwards are from Cairo. (I was going to interject here that Mr. Robinson was the first Egyptian to play Major League baseball, but it would be misinterpreted in this era of political correctness, so I omit the joke.) Festivals dedicated to rattlesnakes, mules, and antique cars are held here annually.

*Unidentifiable hieroglyphics and seemingly abandoned industrial sections of downtown Cairo, above.*

*Right: just a few of the many pyramids to be found in and about Cairo.*

# LEBANON

Lebanon, located just off I-575 north of Atlanta, was, in fact, named for Lebanon which did not become an independent republic until 1964. It was originally called *Toonigh* by the railroad and has pretty much been absorbed by Holly Springs. There is little else to report.

Lebanon, the one which shares its southern border with Israel, has been home to the Phoenicians, then was subsequently conquered and occupied by the Assyrians, the Persians, the Greeks, the Romans, the Arabs, the Crusaders, the Ottoman Turks, and most recently the French. Lebanon, Georgia, has been mostly occupied by Native Americans then Southerners.

The only attractions to get excited about, both pictured here, are the railroad tracks situated in a ravine and what seems to be a bevy of meteorites which perhaps landed near a construction site.

# ARABI

Arabi, near Cordele, was a thriving community in the early 1900s according to reports, although it does not seem to be all that *sheik* today. It had a population then of 505 and, according to the 2000 census, 456 now, so it's almost holding its own, taking the long view. The original settlers met in 1888 to name the railroad stop, and "agreed on this name after a great deal of discussion." It was probably derived from a family name as, outside of Louisiana, there are no other actual places called Arabi, though there should be.

# MADRAS

Madras, probably named for the city in India (now known as Chennai, the capital of Tamil Nadu), was given its name in 1902 by the widow of the man for whom the town was originally named, one George Powell (Powell Station prior). It is near Newnan and was, in the early twentieth century, an important shipping point for folks (for goods, more precisely) in that part of the state. Today it is quite obvious that the community was oriented to the railroad and that it needs another orientation if it is to exist much further into the rest of the twenty-first century.

# BRITISH ISLES

British folk began settling what is now Georgia in February of 1733. General James Oglethorpe and others had secured a charter as trustees for the colony and began settling Anne, now known as Savannah. Part of Oglethorpe's idea for the new settlement was as an alternative to debtor's prison. In 1736 Oglethorpe, recognizing the Spanish threat to the south, recruited Scots, who were willing to take up arms, offering them land and other substantial benefits. They settled in New Inverness, now Darien. This program proved quite beneficial at the 1742 Battle of Bloody Marsh on St. Simons Island. Georgia has always had a problem with people from Florida coming up here causing trouble and that is when it all started. The battle confirmed the British position in Georgia, established by the Treaty of Aix-la-Chapelle. Irish began immigrating to America in the early 1700s settling in Pennsylvania before migrating southward, many to our state. It is no wonder then that there are numerous locations around the state which recognize, by their names, a British heritage.

## DOVER

Let's begin with England and Dover, famous for its white chalk cliffs. Dover, England, is a major ferry port and, ironically, transportation has always been a major endeavor of Dover, Georgia—just north of Statesboro—though rail-oriented. Its entry in the 1906 *Cyclopedia of Georgia* makes it sound like quite the thriving place. It's pretty sleepy these days and the only thing resembling a white cliff would be stacks and stacks of wooden shipping pallets. There is a definite consistency to the architectural style of the buildings there, what few remain.

# ISLE OF WIGHT

To the southeast (in Georgia) near Midway lies the Isle of Wight. The one in England has been a popular resort destination since the Victorian era and has a rich maritime history. It is probably not entirely coincidental that Georgia's Isle of Wight shares similar characteristics, though to a far more modest degree. Queen Victoria, Charles Dickens, and Alfred Lord Tennyson, for example, used to spend summers there. Georgia's has a few summer homes and a deep water B&B. In the maritime department, England's has had sail makers and boat builders for centuries and Hovercraft has a manufacturing plant there while, coincidentally, our's has a place that will repair your outboard motor.

It would appear that it indeed might not be too dear to rent a cottage every summer on the Isle of Wight as was suggested by four young Englishmen a few decades ago as they pondered personal relationships during advancing age and ultimate retirement. (The Beatles? Remember?)

# BATH

A similar amazingly ironic connection can be made in the Baths. Bath, England, is southeast of London and was granted city status in 1590. It was built around the only naturally occurring hot springs in the United Kingdom. Georgia's Bath was settled quite soon after that, in the late 1700s, and became a summer retreat from malaria for Augustinians in the late 1800s. Wealthy planters built elegant summer homes there and took advantage of the therapeutic spring water at the bathhouse. A 1968 article in the *Augusta Chronicle-Herald* mentions the remaining homes and the ruins of the bathhouse. I was unable to spot anything of that era, save a couple of rotting cabins, with the exception of the fine 1784 Presbyterian Church which seems to be thriving. The few residents I queried had not even heard of the baths of Bath. Oh, Bath, England, is a World Heritage Site and has a population of just under 90,000.

# WINDSOR

Let's head west and see what's happening in Windsor. Windsor, Georgia, is precariously close to Atlanta, just outside of Loganville. It was an early settlement and has nothing except for the Windsor Universalist Church which meets once a year, and a solid waste disposal facility across the highway. It was indeed named for the Windsor in England where the castle is and where the most expensive real estate in the UK is situated. These days, it is a buyer's market for real estate in Windsor, Georgia.

# OXFORD

No use spending much time in Windsor, so off we go to Oxford, a short drive south. Oxford, the one in England at any rate, appears in written records as early as 912 and received city status in 1191. It is home to the oldest university in the English-speaking world: Oxford. The connections just don't stop: Oxford, Georgia, is the original home to one of the oldest educational institutions in the South, Emory College (now Oxford College), whose alumni include the Wesley brothers and, continuing a rich heritage, where the *Dukes of Hazzard* opening scene jumps were filmed. The campus respects its English heritage, architecturally, and the town, despite its proximity to a certain large metropolitan area, maintains a pleasant small town atmosphere. This is also, ironically, where Tony Blair practices law.

# MANCHESTER

Our whirlwind tour of England continues in the greater Manchester area. The industrial revolution got its first toehold in Manchester which quickly became a textile manufacturing center and grew from township to city status in just a few decades. During the Victorian era it was referred to as "Cottonopolis" and in 1913, sixty-five percent of the world's cotton was processed in the greater Manchester area. Manchester, Georgia, was named for its English counterpart and was chosen in 1917 as the confluent point of three railroads making it quite the transportation hub.

Bowdon, England, is a residential community within the Manchester area. It seems to have been one of the first bedroom communities in the world with a rail station built in 1849 providing service to downtown Manchester. I would like to report that Bowdon, Georgia, similarly lies just outside Manchester, Georgia. Unfortunately, it is a two hour drive to the northwest (but very close to Ephesus which we visited earlier on).

# BOWDON

Bowdon, Georgia, *The Friendly City,* was named, not after its British counterpart, but after a senator from Alabama of all things. It was incorporated in 1859. In 1860, the census reported a population of some 304 which has swelled to a staggering 2000 in a mere 149 years! Of the similar small towns in Georgia, its downtown area seems to be thriving more than most with storefronts containing artist's studios, techie businesses, and the like.

*The British flag does not fly in the friendly city of Bowdon.*

# BRISTOL

Bristol, Georgia, was originally called Lightsey after Jack Lightsey. Then Lem Lightsey came along and renamed it Bristol, indeed after the one in England. Bristol is England's sixth most populous city and received its Royal Charter in 1155. Coincidentally, Georgia's lost its charter on July 1, 1995. Bristol, England, is a major seaport, a trading and cultural center, and plays a significant role in the aerospace, information technology, finance and defense industries, characteristics not shared by its south Georgia counterpart.

*Above right, Bristol's residential district. Note the bifurcated chimney, an architectural feature unique to the Bristol vernacular.*

*Right, Bristol's industrial district.*

*Opposite page, Bristol's commercial district.*

# EPWORTH

Epworth, in the foothills of the Appalachian mountains, was originally called Atalla. The Reverend Alexander Haren organized a Methodist church there in 1865. Later Methodists started a seminary which they named Epworth after John Wesley's birthplace. The Post Office wisely followed suit.

Characteristics the Epworths share, John and Charles Wesley aside, are pretty much limited to size: both are small. (An accompanying photograph clearly indicates this to be a one horse town.)

The spring shown here is on the grounds of the Methodist church. It was a vital source of water for Methodist campers and their horses and cows in the 1800s. The owner fenced it in leaving the Methodists dry. They prayed for a water supply and that night, during a storm, the spring relocated outside the fence onto church property. A monument declares it to be "providentially given" to the church and who, I ask, would argue?

# Scotland

Scotland is but briefly represented in the Peach State, so let's knock it out before spending time in Ireland. First we have Scotland, named after the preponderance of settlers from, well, Scotland. If you're taking the 341 route to Atlanta from the southern coast and are not in a rush, it would be worth taking the small detour to Scotland, just before you get to McRae, to see what a small railroad town in Georgia must have looked like at the turn of the century (the other turn). The preeminent structure is the old brick post office, now sadly abandoned. It had some manufacturing and shipping concerns in 1900 but commercial activity seems to be limited now to a few retail establishments and a couple of diners. Perhaps a haggis is available in one. No kilts nor bagpipes were noted on my two brief visits to the community.

*Several breeds of dogs originated in Scotland, the country, including Golden Retriever, Border Collie, Scottish Terrier, Shetland Sheepdog, and Scottish Deerhound. Above, a purebred Georgian Scottish Dawg.*

# DUBLIN

Ireland has fared much better in the state of Georgia. Dublin was named for the hometown of the wife of one Jonathan Sawyer who donated the land for the public buildings, as, of course, would have been his prerogative. The 1907 *Cyclopedia* describes it as quite the thriving metropolis with rail traffic and river traffic and all manners of industry. The town celebrates its Irish heritage with a St. Patrick's festival in March and its Southern heritage with the Redneck Games in the summer. I wanted to get a picture of the inside of an "Irish Pub" with its inhabitants, and the one shown here was perfect, but the elderly bartender wouldn't give me permission as the owner was absent. When I returned, a few weeks later, the place had sadly been razed.

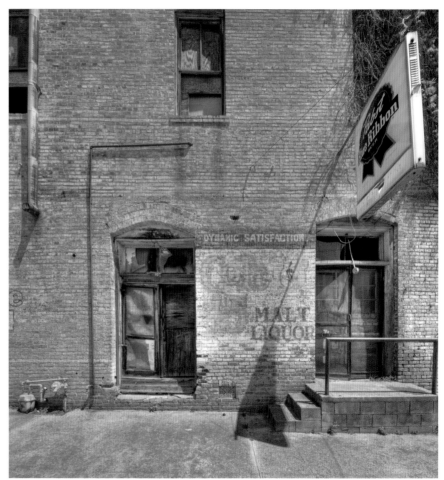

*Preparing for the festival*

*An Irish pub*

*A celebration of local fauna, opposite page*

# BELFAST

Off to Belfast. There do not appear to have been any major partisan disputes in Belfast, Georgia, such have been endured for so long in its namesake, unless you count a revolutionary war affair wherein a Patriot commander captured some Torys during their dinner and exchanged them for a captured colonel. The accompanying photograph depicts all the remnants of *the troubles* I could find in Belfast.

# CORK

Let's pop over to Cork which was originally named Dublin and originally settled by Irish. It began as a trading and shipping center for Butts county. In that regard, the most you can give it today is that there is, indeed, a railroad track nearby. The photograph dramatically captures Cork's entire commercial district.

# Limerick

Let's see what Limerick has to offer. It, too, was a shipping port in its heyday. It was named by immigrants after, of course, the town in Ireland. Today, it is not that easy to find and has but a bunch of houses there and one convenience store. Its Irish counterpart currently has a gang problem, but that seems not to be a contemporary issue in Georgia, not in Limerick at any rate. Captured here are examples of traditional Limerick architecture, local fauna, and the remnants of some long-forgotten transportation system.

# KILDARE

Kildare, Ireland, is home to the Irish National Stud, Japanese Garden, and St. Fiachra's garden. Kildare, Georgia, is not even mentioned in any historical resource at my disposal. The photograph captures the entirety of Kildare: a small store there with tolerable coffee and absolutely nothing to distinguish its Irish heritage, unless ennui is a particularly Irish trait.

# KILLARNEY

I am excited as I travel to Killarney. It is the weekend before St. Patrick's Day and the real Killarney is known as a popular tourist destination and party town! My Killarney experience proved to be a different story. It's pretty much these days a farm and contrasts markedly with its counterpart in Ireland, unless the cattle I saw there get crazy after sundown. It seems to be but one farm–a very nice farm–and an appropriately hued green, if abandoned, house. I leave the place, disappointingly sober.

# THE CONTINENT

## AMSTERDAM

If you're interested in seeing canals or red light districts, the Amsterdam in Georgia is not for you. Let me be frank, if you're interested in seeing *anything*, Amsterdam, Georgia is not for you. In its heyday, the late 1800s and early 1900s, Amsterdam was the largest singly-held tobacco plantation in the whole world, and had, at one time, a population of 450. Today, it can't be far into the double digits if that. The only tourist attraction, mysteriously denoted with a "no trespassing" sign, is an abandoned diner or club.

An actual, if oblique, connection is one Eagle Bill (1942-2005), *a native of rural Georgia* who invented the vaporizer, an alternative technology for partaking of cannabis products. He was for over a decade himself an actual exhibit at the Hemp, Hash, & Marijuana Museum located at Oudezijdsachterburgwal 148, Amsterdam, but unfortunately it's the one in the Netherlands.

*Amsterdam's residential district*

*Amsterdam's agricultural district*

# Harlem

Harlem is another railroad town which was incorporated in 1870. It was named after the then-fashionable suburb of New York which pre-dates our Harlem by over 200 years. It in turn was named by Peter Styvesant after Holland's Haarlem. Georgia's Harlem is the birthplace of none other than Oliver Hardy who appeared in over four hundred films, many with Stan Laurel. Could it be merely an historic coincidence that Mr. Hardy's career got underway during the early years of the Harlem Renaissance, or could there be a Georgia-based component to the movement? And could it be another coincidence that Haarlem's Cinema Palace, one of the oldest movie theatres in Holland, was established exactly the same time Oliver Hardy's movie career was beginning? Either way, *it is a fine mess* and I leave it to you, dear reader, to ponder these mysteries.

# Denmark

Denmark, Georgia, is another one of the hamlets for which very little information is available other than it was named for the country. It could be because there is very little to know about in the first place. The railroad missed it by several miles which would have deprived it of a catalyst for development in the early days. The late twentieth century seems to have been as equally parsimonious toward the community.

# Geneva

Geneva, Georgia, settled before 1840, was indeed named for the city in Switzerland. It was originally called Koockogey, so *Geneva* would have been a welcome improvement. It is not readily apparent what the Switzerland connection might be. There are no large mountains nearby, no treaties have been negotiated. There is, ironically, a lake in town (pictured to the right)—that will have to suffice. According to the *Cyclopedia* it was somewhat of a shipping center in 1900. To an outside observer it has since lost this distinction.

*Geneva's entertainment district, above. Right: icons of religion and twenty-first century technology exist side-by-side.*

# ALPS

Alps, about half way between Atlanta and Columbus, is another Georgia community that does not seem to exist anymore nor is there much evidence to suggest that it ever did. The terrain is somewhat hilly which could suggest an Alpine environment to an imaginative person who had never visited Switzerland, Austria, or northern Italy. As depicted in the accompanying photographs, it seems to be abandoned.

# WATERLOO

Waterloo is located just a few miles south of Seville, the Georgia one, of course. Little-to-no historic information is easily accessible, but according to Mr. Krakow's book, it was "supposedly named by Joe Young who bought up property here, and afterwards his business deals went bad and he 'met his Waterloo.'" This reference is, of course, made to the 1815 battle in present-day Belgium which terminated Napoleon's rule as Emperor of the French. So the Georgia community is not so much named after a location, but rather an idiomatic expression. A cursory observation would deem it not inappropriately denoted as it appears that, the presence of a small church notwithstanding, Waterloo may have similarly met its *Waterloo*.

# SPAIN

One would never accidentally find one's self in Spain, Georgia. It is hard enough to find even if you're looking for it, which the normal person would not. But as I reluctantly progress down a dirt road just after sunup, in fog, I imagine an iconic image for Spain. The first thing that comes to mind is the bullfight. I finally arrive at the intersection that my Gazetteer indicates as Spain. The irony is palpable. The only characteristic differentiating Spain from the past five miles of south Georgia is a field full of cows, with a bull present no less. And it is plain. And rain is falling. Another example of the extreme irony of realities exposed by this odd-yssey. I shoot the bull, then head on my way—there is much more ground to cover.

# Seville

Seville, Spain, is the artistic, cultural, and financial capital of southern Spain with a population of just under 1.5 million. Its cuisine is based on seafood, olive oil, and sherry, all produced in surrounding provinces. It is the primary setting of many operas including Rossini's *The Barber of Seville*, Bizet's *Carmen*, Verdi's *La Forza del Destino*, Beethoven's *Fidelio*, as well as Mozart's *Don Giovanni* and *The Marriage of Figaro*. It is the Rossini work I would presently call your attention to.

Seville, Georgia, was a thriving lumber, turpentine, and shipping town in the day. It became unincorporated, sadly, in 1995. There are a number of houses there today along with a formerly beautiful, abandoned church building, abandoned warehouses, and a couple of abandoned commercial and agricultural storage buildings. There is but one open business in the whole town (whose population in 1900 stood at 1,277). It is Jo Friel's Shear Outlooks Salon (opposite page). This is nearly beyond belief: the only ongoing business concern in all of Seville is a barber. (It's a salon, if you want to split hairs, but *The Barber of Seville* reference is just far too ironic to ignore.)

Seville, Georgia, was indeed named after the city in Spain, and you can bet your tapas they are not pronounced identically.

# Vienna

Vienna, Georgia, mispronounced as most southern towns, especially Georgia's, was named for the capitol of Austria. It was a thriving, bustling place in the late 1800s processing cotton and lumber products. Some of the cotton part of that activity remains today. The city's web site boasts of its downtown renovation, and it has been recognized as a "City of Excellence," and I do not mean to demean the efforts, but the murals painted on walls downtown depict a Vienna history which, frankly, is more romantic than the current condition of the buildings upon which they are painted. Granted, Vienna has done a much better job of maintaining its presence than, say, a Sparta or a Milan, but it is unfortunate that we have allowed our formerly charming downtowns, small or large, to decay and collapse. External economic activity controls these events. It was the development of the railroad system during the mid-to-late 1800s that gave birth to many of these communities in Georgia. Small towns that still rely on industries that are serviced by rail, or where former presidents used to vacation, remain in the best condition. Small towns, where the trains no longer stop, tend to be the crumbling and abandoned ones. Later, the Interstate system was built which introduced a whole new dynamic to economic activity, further eroding the viability of many small downtowns which were bypassed by the I-95s and I-75s and the I-20s.

# Sweden

There are several places in Georgia which are referred to in Mr. Krakaw's book as "a former community." Sweden is one of these. When you arrive at it where it is shown to be on a map, you do not realize that you are somewhere. Located just south of Carter's Lake, it is in a region of what passes as mountainous in the state of Georgia, and was named for the Scandinavian country, perhaps because of the scenery.

# BUDAPEST/NITRA

In the late 1880s, Ralph Spencer of Haralson County organized the Georgia Fruit Growing and Winery Association and convinced some fifty Hungarian families (who had knowledge of winemaking) to relocate from Pennsylvania where they had been mining coal. The operation was successful and by 1900 some two hundred families had moved in. They named their community Budapest. Just down the road some Slovaks had also moved in for the same purposes and called their hamlet Nitra which, at its peak, had sixty houses and a general store.

In addition to winemaking, the immigrants had brought all their other skills with them from the old country, bread and cheese making for example. The communities flourished. They built their own Catholic church, rectory, and a school.

Sadly, 1908 eventually arrived (around 1908) and with it Prohibition. This put an end to activities in Budapest and Nitra and the residents were forced to move elsewhere to seek employment. (The red clay is apparently not good for much else.) Traveling today on Highway 78, there is nothing to suggest that you are in or near an historic community.

# GERMANY

Owing to emigration history, Germany is well represented in the state of Georgia. What more appropriate place to begin than in Germany. Germany, Georgia, is located just west of Clayton in north Georgia adjacent to the Chattahoochee National Forest. It is a spot on the map, but not in the actual landscape. I guess it's more of an idea than a municipality.

# HAMBURG

Hamburg State Park was named after Hamburg, South Carolina, which was named by its founder, Henry Shultz in 1821, after his hometown of, you guessed it, Hamburg, Germany. The restored and operating grist mill there (on Hamburg Lake) dates from 1921 and the park is a very nice park. (Hamburg, Germany, with its system of rivers, streams, and canals, has more bridges within its city limits than any other city in the world and, true to form, our Hamburg has a significant water feature.)

# BERLIN

Berlin, a now-faltering agricultural center in south Georgia, was indeed named after the German capitol. Interestingly, the name was changed to Lens during World War I but reverted afterwards. According to the web site, berlin.georgia.gov, there is a festival in October, but it's not even in Berlin. It is in far-off Moultrie which is beyond the scope of this present venture. I explore downtown Berlin nonetheless and am not disappointed. I can now say in all sincerity, "Ich bin ein Berliner." Braunschweig is a short drive up the Autobahn, or US 84 depending on the route you choose.

*Technology peeks out from behind a modest shed near the spot where President Ronald Reagan famously implored, "Mr. Gorbachev, tear down this store!"*

# BRUNSWICK

Brunswick, Georgia, could just as easily have been placed in the British Isles section of this *book,* but the ultimate reference is German, and it gets a tad complicated, so here it is. Georgia was named in honor of King George II of England. Brunswick, founded in 1771, was named in honor of his son, King George III, (the grandfather of Queen Victoria). How? Well, all of the King Georges were of the House of Hanover, a German royal dynasty which ruled the Duchy of Brunswick-Lüneburg, the Kingdom of Hanover, the Kingdom of Great Britain, and the Kingdom of Ireland. This also explains all the George and Hanover references in downtown Brunswick.

Brunswick, in German, is Braunschweig which is where Braunschweiger comes from. It makes a superior sandwich in the opinion of this author, especially when paired with a slice of Vidalia onion (grown just a few miles north), a slice of Meünster cheese, and a good brown mustard on fresh pumpernickel bread, but that is beyond the scope of the current work. Braunschweig is home to the Schimmel and Steinway piano companies and, in a rare coincidence, Brunswick has Jamestown Piano Shop where you can actually get yourself a Steinway. Brunswick has always been an important port city, in fact that is one of its nicknames, and today, in an inadvertent nod to history, several German auto exports enter the U.S. through this port.

In all fairness, Willie's Wee-Nee Wagon does not serve Braunschweiger sausage and Brunswick has a lot going for it—not depicted herein— an excellent symphony orchestra for example as well as a thriving and quickly expanding local college. This book was obviously not commissioned by anyone's Chamber of Commerce.

# DRESDEN

Dresden, Georgia, is a "place" near Newnan. Dresden, Germany, is a city the Allied Forces leveled during World War II. Kurt Vonnegut was there as a POW and recounts the experience in his novel *Slaughterhouse Five*. This is relevant because there is nothing in Dresden, Georgia: it seems to be merely the convergent point for several power lines. As with several communities in this leg of our Odd-yssey, no useful historic information exists for Dresden, Georgia. The photograph (right) would suggest that it is probably not an ideal location for kite flying.

# HANOVER

My sources report that Hanover is the site of the second largest Oktoberfest. Unfortunately, my brief visit was in March, near St. Patrick's Day, so I missed the festivities. All that was visible to the casual observer was a small cluster of green, empty, uninspired buildings with a bumper crop of yellow bollards. King George III, in charge during the settling of Georgia, was of the House of Hanover, but I have no empirical data to suggest these names are related.

# BREMEN

Bremen, Georgia, the "clothing center of the South," was incorporated in 1883. It was in fact named for the German seaport. It had been named Kramer after a German immigrant – Herr Kramer presumably – who had a nearby vineyard, but he requested the change. Bremen, the one in Germany, is a major transportation and industrial center. The two municipalities are eerily connected: as I was setting up a photograph of a factory, an Amtrak train, the *Crescent*, came through on its way to New Orleans. Industry and transportation, just like the old country. (Amtrak does not actually stop in Bremen, but that is not germane to this discussion.)

# Rhine

Rhine was incorporated in 1891 and was settled by Germans who were, in fact, from the Rhine River area. It, too, is on the railroad, the next stop past Milan in fact, and was quite the shipping center in the late 1800s, there being turpentine and lumber production flourishing. The Ocmulgee River is nearby, so there's your other ironic connection to the German Rhine. There is a building downtown which derives from an obvious Bavarian aesthetic. The Rhine, of course, is on the other side of Germany and home to stone castles perched on cliffs overlooking the river, but whoever built it must be commended for at least getting the country right. (There is also a grand Italianate villa on the main road going out of town which you don't want to get caught photographing: inquisitive people in pickup trucks will approach you faster than *bianco* on *risotto*.)

# ITALY

## TURIN

Odyfferus finds himself in Italy, a country surprisingly well represented in Georgia. First stop: Turin. Turin, Italy, is a manufacturing city in northern Italy and is known as Italy's Detroit. It is also home to the famous–if controversial–shroud. Turin, Georgia, was originally known as Location. (Imagine the conversations that may have disrupted: Where are you from? Location. Yes, location, where you're from. Yes. Yes, what? This may have been the inspiration for the famous "Who's on First" routine.)

In the early 1900s Turin had "important mercantile and shipping interests" which are all but gone. It is the site, however, of what could easily become one of the most popular tourist attractions in the whole state if the Coweta County Visitors and Tourism Bureau would wake up. Barbie Beach lies on the main highway and has probably caused accidents. The owners of the property were inspired to build it after Georgia Power killed the roses growing in the easement. The diorama changes themes with holidays and news events, but its default setting is a clothing-optional beach with volleyball and Kens who may or may not be all that interested in Barbies, if you get my meaning.

The most fascinating aspect of the roadside attraction, in the context of this Odd-yssey, is the backdrop hanging on the clothesline at the rear. It is comprised of several shrouds. Well, they look like shrouds, I would call them shrouds.

*Opposite page: pilgrims stop to pay their respects to Barbie Beach.*

# Milan

Milan is Italy's second largest city and regarded as one of the world's design and fashion capitals. If Milan, Georgia, is to be regarded as the capital of anything, it better take advantage soon, as its downtown is literally crumbling.

Milan is a railroad town incorporated in 1891. The wife of the railroad executive who was constructing the town had just returned from a trip to Milan and loved it and that was the inspiration for the name. (Keeping true to Georgia standards, the name is mispronounced.)

The two blocks of buildings which comprise downtown was at one time a bustling place. One can tell that more than a little thought went into the design of it: the bank has huge, stately columns, the overall scale is perfect for pedestrians, the north end of the street is enclosed by old railroad buildings (now the police station), and the theatre used to be the community hot spot on Friday nights. Young people are not returning to Milan anymore, according to the bank president (who came out to see why someone would be photographing his bank). In fact, he hadn't planned to himself. His father was the owner of the pile of bricks on the next block which, when they were properly assembled until recently, served as the town's grocery store. Milan's chief of police (who owns a store and also drove up to see why someone would be photographing his building) is also the chief of police of nearby Rhine.

*Milan's theatre district*

*Milan's former downtown grocery store lies in ruins, a fact that one could call thoughtless, even rude.*

*Milan's financial district*

# VALDOSTA

Valdosta, known as *The Azalea City, Vale of Beauty,* and *Naval Stores Capital of the World,* was named for one of Governor George Troup's plantations. There was a Troupville, but it was four miles away from where the railroad was to be routed, so a new town was established (in 1860) and they wanted to keep a Troup reference. What is fuzzy is the derivation of Valdosta. Some say it is from "val de osta" which, in Italian, supposedly translates to "beautiful valley." Others say it means "vale of beauty." What is not fuzzy is that there is a region in northern Italy called "Valle d'Aosta," an area noted for skiing and where you go to see Mont Blanc and the Matterhorn. It was a Roman outpost around 25 BC and the name "Aosta" is probably an Italian corruption of "Augustus" (a lot can happen in two thousand years). Why the governor would name a farm in south Georgia this is anyone's guess.

Georgia's, regardless of etymology, is quite a charming little city, though one is hard pressed to find any reference to an Alp or a Matterhorn. The courthouse is mildly Italianate I suppose. Valdosta State University is located here and there are still naval store references on old signs painted on a few brick buildings downtown.

Adjacent to the university campus is, indeed, a small beautiful valley in a park, pictured here.

# THE NEW WORLD

## BERMUDA

We have several new world islands to explore, so let's sail over to Bermuda and see what it has in store. Not much as it turns out. Bermuda is another one of those "post-hamlets" for which there is little to no historic information readily available. It can be stated with impunity, however, that it lies about twenty five miles west of Albany and is about that far northeast of Damascus which we explored earlier. Bermudan architecture seems to be strangely rooted in an agrarian, non-island aesthetic as clearly illustrated in the photographs.

# JAMAICA

In 1900, Jamaica, defined now as the spot where a dirt road crosses a railroad track, was inhabited by some seventy two, had an express office, and some "mercantile interests." Today, some 110 years later, it does not appear to have a population and any commercial interests would seem to be limited to the export of venison. Before you start getting your Bob Marley recordings out, be advised that Jamaica was named after the home—in New York—of one of the Atlantic Coastline Railroad investors. As is obvious in the photographs, Jamaican architecture seems to be limited to a hunting aesthetic.

# CUBA

In spite of U.S. imposed travel restrictions, I manage to get into Cuba easily and am not impeded in any way with my documentary endeavors. I chat with a friendly local who, while quite fluent in English, cannot tell me how Cuba got its name. According to Mr. Krakow, it was settled in 1875 and so-named because it, like Castro's Cuba, is surrounded by water and noted for swamps. That's fine, but there are lots of swampy places in the world, so why Cuba specifically? It would seem to be run by Presbyterians. The mystery of its pedigree continues only half-solved and I leave without a cigar.

# MONTEZUMA

Our travels take us now to Montezuma, just south of Macon, which we could easily reach by rail. Montezuma, incorporated in 1854, was, according to some accounts, named by Aztec descendants, or by soldiers returning from the Mexican-American War. Its development has been based on transportation, from stagecoach ferries in the 1700s, to rail, and to steamboats on the Flint River. Montezuma was missed several miles by the newfangled Interstate, so it, like many other small towns, struggles for survival. It possesses a downtown with a distinct urban character and still, in these trying times, a relatively vibrant quality about it.

With a constant stream of rail traffic, it must be amazing how much freight a train hauls through Montezuma.

Downtown is anchored to the north by a temple-like building surrounded by columns, not unlike the Parthenon, or, at least, a cheap imitation of the Parthenon. It is for sale. Another predominant entity is a Mexican restaurant called, appropriately, "Mexican Restaurant." I must ask: would you eat without hesitation in a town called Montuzuma in a Mexican restaurant called "Mexican Restaurant?" Nope, me neither.

# HALIFAX

Halifax is a spot on the map up the Satilla River on the outskirts of Woodbine in Camden County. Henry Ellis, the second royal governor of Georgia, was appointed to his position by Lord Halifax in 1757. Ellis did a good job in resolving several conflicts which had arisen during the first governorship including settling the claims of Mary Musgrove and in 1760 was subsequently awarded the governorship of Nova Scotia where there is also a city named Halifax. I am going out on a limb to suggest that perhaps these names are all related somehow. In the late 1800s Georgia rivers were dotted with saw mills and docks from which in-demand Georgia lumber was shipped, primarily for use in shipbuilding up north. There would have been nothing to sustain a small community after the trees were all chopped down and shipped away, so many of these places, Halifax included, are now remnants. It was related to me, in Halifax, that many men who had never been on a ship showed up for work at the dock in Halifax, were bought overalls by a captain, and they were instant sailors who took their cargo to the northern Halifax.

*From the approximate spot where the Halifax wharf would have been, Interstate 95, the now-preferred route for moving freight to New England, is visible about a mile away.*

# CEYLON

Just a couple of miles downstream from Halifax is Ceylon which was named after the island which is now Sri Lanka. Its history and current disposition parallel that of Halifax to a tea. It was part of an original King's grant made to an early member of the Lang family. (The Lang family is big in southeast Georgia.) The first Lang raised horses and was killed in a tragic horse accident on the property. Some of the original acreage today is occupied by Lang's descendents who have recently reintroduced equine endeavors to the property. Sri Lanka (Ceylon) is famous for the production and export of tea and it must be noted here that sweet tea is an extremely popular beverage in south Georgia. It is even called "the house wine of the South." Coincidence? Could South Georgia be the original port of entry for what ultimately became Sweet Tea?

# Australia

## Queensland

All journeys must eventually come to an end, and the present one will wrap up in Queensland. I have never seen a kangaroo before, so imagine my disappointment when I find there nothing but churches. Queensland must have the highest per capita incidence of churches of anywhere in the civilised world. Historically, this is another community for which no data is available except that it is in Ben Hill County.

# AFTERWORD

On his tumultuous return trip home after the war with Troy, Odysseus encountered Lotus Eaters, Cyclops, ill winds, cannibals, a witch-goddess, Sirens, a six-headed monster, a shipwreck, and Calypso–a seductress–who diverted Odysseus's attentions for some seven years! For good or bad, the goddess Athena asked Zeus to intervene. He sent Hermes (the gods' messenger) to persuade Calypso to release Odysseus so he could return to his wife, Penelope, and family, and Ithaca, his home, as mentioned at the beginning of the present opus.

When he finally gets back, he is disguised as a beggar and discovers that a bunch of suitors are hanging around his house doing whatever suitors do which, of course, is not desirable. An archery contest is devised which Odysseus (still disguised as a beggar) wins by shooting an arrow through a dozen axe heads and then turns around and does the same to the assembled suitors. (He is, by the way, assisted by the gods on a number of occasions which, it could easily be argued, gives him an unfair advantage in the resolution of his conflicts.) A few more unsavory things occur before the *Odyssey* finally, thankfully, ends.

How I long for such excitement, challenge and drama. Our twenty-first century *Odd-yssey* through international Georgia is now complete and, as compared to the tale related by Homer, is fairly uneventful and relatively anticlimactic. Absent any form of excitement, Odyfferus and I hope you have found the Georgia journey at least somewhat informative and entertaining.

As witnessed in the previous hundred and some-odd pages, Georgia obviously has a rich history and heritage. An admittedly limited, but significant segment of its present condition is documented here and its future is up for grabs. Several locations in this book are officially defined as "former communities." What a shame it would be for an entire state's remaining historically and architecturally significant resources (buildings and whole towns) be allowed to fall into an irreparable state based solely on temporal economic factors. Further discussion of this topic is beyond the scope of the present work, being couched primarily in ironic historical fiction (a new discipline invented here).

I do not actually suggest your own *odd-yssey* based on this work but, next time you are making a major drive someplace, consider allowing an extra hour or two and take the "blue highways" instead of the Interstate and experience the real Georgia, its real people, and its real history. Slow down a little. Stop at a family-owned BBQ joint instead of a fast food franchise. Get a snack at a farmer's roadside stand instead of a convenient store. (They tend to have good boiled p-nuts.) Meet and experience the real, if disappearing, Georgia and help keep it alive.